ROALD
AMUNDSEN

Please visit our web site at: **www.worldalmanaclibrary.com**
For a free color catalog describing World Almanac® Library's list of high-quality books
and multimedia programs, call 1-800-848-2928 (USA) or 1-800-387-3178 (Canada).
World Almanac® Library's fax: (414) 332-3567.

Library of Congress Cataloging-in-Publication Data

Broderick, Enid.
        Roald Amundsen / by Enid Broderick. — North American ed.
            p. cm. — (Great explorers)
        Includes bibliographical references and index.
        Summary: Reviews the life and expeditions of the Norwegian explorer who first
reached the South Pole, with emphasis on the criticism some of his decisions received.
Includes photographs taken during his expeditions.
        ISBN 0-8368-5011-4 (lib. bdg.)
        ISBN 0-8368-5171-4 (softcover)
        1. Amundsen, Roald, 1872-1928—Juvenile literature. 2. Explorers—Norway—
Biography—Juvenile literature. 3. Polar regions—Discovery and exploration—Juvenile
literature. [1. Amundsen, Roald, 1872-1928. 2. Explorers. 3. Polar regions—
Discovery and exploration.] I. Title. II. Great explorers (Milwaukee, Wis.)
        G585.A6B76   2001
        919.804'092—dc21
        [B]   2001026963

This North American edition first published in 2002 by
World Almanac® Library
330 West Olive Street, Suite 100
Milwaukee, Wisconsin 53212 USA

This U.S. edition © 2002 by World Almanac® Library.
Created with original © 2001 by Quartz Editions,
112 Station Road, Edgware HA8 7AQ, U.K.
Additional end matter © 2002 by World Almanac® Library.

Series Editor: Tamara Green
World Almanac® Library editor and contributing writer: Gini Holland
World Almanac® Library project editor: Betsy Rasmussen
World Almanac® Library designer: Melissa Valuch

The creators and publishers of this volume wish to thank the following for their kind permission to feature
illustration material: Front cover: main image, Helen Jones/ other images, Natural History Photographic Agency/
Tony Stone Images/ National Maritime Museum, Greenwich/Amundsen Collection/ Stuart Brendon/ AKG; Back
cover: AKG/ Royal Geographical Society/ Natural History Photographic Agency/ Mary Evans Picture Library; 5 t
AKG/ c, b Tony Stone Images; 6 t Bridgeman Art Library/ c, b Natural History Photographic Agency; 7 Helen
Jones; 8 t Bridgeman Art Library/ b Natural History Photographic Agency; 10 t National Maritime Museum,
Greenwich / c Oxford Scientific Films/ b Natural History Photographic Agency; 11 t Royal Geographical Society/
b Science & Society Picture Library; 12-13 Stuart Brendon; 14 Amundsen Collection; 15 Science & Society
Picture Library; 16 Amundsen Collection; 17 t AKG/ b Natural History Photographic Agency; 18 t Natural
History Photographic Agency/ b Bridgeman Art Library, Royal Geographical Society; 19 t AKG/ b Natural History
Photographic Agency; 20 The Art Archive; 21 t Amundsen Collection/ c, b Natural History Photographic Agency;
22-25 Amundsen Collection; 26 t Mary Evans Picture Library/ b Ancient Art & Architecture Collection; 27 Mary
Evans Picture Library; 28 t Royal Geographical Society/ c, b AKG; 30 t Tony Stone Images/ c Royal Geographical
Society/ b Amundsen Collection; 31 t Royal Geographical Society/ b Amundsen Collection; 32 t Bridgeman Art
Library/ c Amundsen Collection/ b Natural History Photographic Agency; 33 t Amundsen Collection/ c Royal
Geographical Society/ b AKG; 34 t AKG/ b Bridgeman Art Library; 35 t Bridgeman Art Library/ c National
Portrait Gallery, London /b National Maritime Museum, Greenwich; 36 AKG; 38 t AKG/ c Natural History
Photographic Agency/ b Bridgeman Art Library, Scott Polar Research Institute; 39 t Bridgeman Art Library, Royal
Geographical Society/ c, b Natural History Photographic Agency; 40 t AKG/ c Science & Society Picture Library/
b Natural History Photographic Agency; 42 Bridgeman Art Library; 43 Helen Jones

Printed in the United States of America

1 2 3 4 5 6 7 8 9 06 05 04 03 02

ROALD
AMUNDSEN

ENID BRODERICK

WORLD ALMANAC® LIBRARY

CONTENTS

INTRODUCTION

A skilled skier who grew up near the Arctic Circle in Norway, Amundsen (*right*) self-trained to achieve his goals.

ROALD AMUNDSEN dared to explore the Arctic and Antarctic regions. He successfully navigated the Northwest Passage and raced to become first to reach the South Pole.

It was difficult and dangerous to navigate around large icebergs (*above*).

Roald Amundsen was born into a wealthy shipowning family. His mother wanted him to become a doctor, but his own ambition to become a polar explorer started early. As a boy, Amundsen read everything he could about previous polar explorations. As he grew older, he began to prepare himself to be physically and mentally ready to succeed in dangerous and challenging situations. He worked hard physically to strengthen his body. He developed skills in ocean navigation, fishing, seal hunting, and dog handling. He got licensed as an airplane pilot and ship's skipper.

Huskies (*below*) pulled the dog sleds that helped Amundsen race to the South Pole.

As an adult from the late 1800s into the early 1900s, Amundsen achieved many triumphs as an explorer, but his character was often called into question. He frequently told lies or withheld information in order to gain the financial support he needed. These same lies, combined with his competitive drive to be first, often led to disagreements and quarrels with other explorers of his time. His work was, however, valued in his time and has been remembered in ours. The polar regions he explored and mapped have given us information about those areas' plants, animals, and topography, as well as an understanding of our global climate.

ROALD AMUNDSEN

MAN OF AMBITION

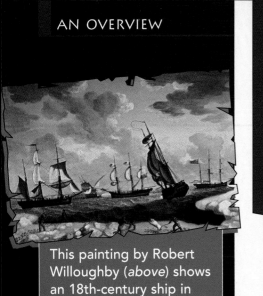

This painting by Robert Willoughby (*above*) shows an 18th-century ship in Arctic waters. Amundsen was inspired by such images as a boy.

Photographed during a Norwegian autumn, this house (*below*) once belonged to Amundsen.

Due to Amundsen's achievement, there is now an international research base at the South Pole (*below*).

Roald Amundsen, who liked to call himself "the last of the Vikings," was both the first to navigate the Northwest Passage and the first to reach the South Pole.

The youngest child of a wealthy shipowner, Roald Amundsen was born on July 16, 1872, in the small town of Borge, near Christiania, as the capital of Norway (now Oslo) was then known. As a boy, he loved all kinds of sports, particularly soccer.

Since Norway straddles the snowbound Arctic Circle, Amundsen, like many Norwegians, became an excellent skier as a youth. He took a special interest in ski equipment, studying what kinds of skis and waxes would improve his speed in various snow conditions. He worked hard to develop his skill and endurance. In fact, Amundsen's skiing ability and interest were so intense that his boyhood friends gave him the childhood nickname "Arctic Explorer." Little did they know how accurate that nickname would become.

The climate of Norway provided a perfect training ground for Amundsen; he always slept with his bedroom window wide open, working to build a strong constitution. Amundsen also practiced gymnastics as part of an intensive bodybuilding program. This helped prepare him for the demanding physical challenges of Arctic and Antarctic exploration he would encounter as an adult.

When Amundsen was young, he and many Norwegians took an interest

> **"I also wanted to suffer for a cause — not in a burning desert on the way to Jerusalem — but in the frosty North."**

in the ongoing mapping of uncharted Arctic territory. At age 14, he read about the failed expedition of British navy captain Sir John Franklin, who struggled to find the Northwest Passage in 1845. Franklin had perished with all his crew in the freezing wilderness. After reading this, Amundsen decided that he would succeed where Franklin had failed. He would become a polar explorer who was prepared for all the physical and mental challenges the Arctic wilderness could present.

FAMILY TRAGEDIES

Amundsen's plans were spoiled almost immediately. His father died, and his grieving mother wanted her youngest to study medicine. This was frustrating for Amundsen, but to please his

Amundsen (*right*) was equally comfortable both in the homes of wealthy supporters who helped finance his expeditions and when camping in frozen polar regions. He was also at ease on land, at sea, and in the air. He trained as a sea captain, and in 1914, he became the first Norwegian to earn his pilot's license.

mother, he began to study at Norway's Christiania University in 1891. Since he was from a wealthy family, he lived well, even while a student, and was known for his fashionable clothes and enjoyment of fine living.

Then tragedy struck again. In 1893, when Amundsen was 21 and halfway though his studies, his mother suddenly died.

A portion of Amundsen's own manuscript draft for his autobiography (*below*). He was well-organized, in both his words and his actions.

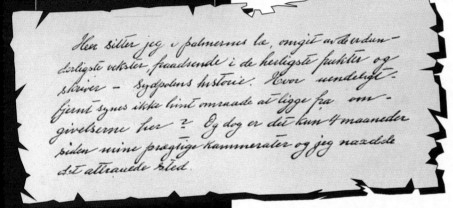

A memorial at Spitsbergen, Norway (*right*), marks Amundsen's unsuccessful attempt to reach the North Pole with Ellsworth in 1925.

He left the university without finishing his schooling. He decided it was time to follow his dream.

LOCKED IN ICE

All through his teens, he had read every account of polar expeditions that he could find. All of them had failed in some way, and Amundsen realized their common mistake. These polar explorers, lacking sailing skills, had always relied on sea captains. He noted that these expeditions suffered from having two leaders, the captain and the explorer, who often quarreled and divided the crew.

So that he could learn to captain a boat, he joined the Norwegian navy in 1894. He also signed up on an Arctic sailing ship to get his skipper's license, in the summers of 1874 through 1876. This ship hunted seals in the Arctic Ocean. While the slaughter appalled him, he gained valuable experience.

He learned to navigate through polar ice and to hunt at sea. Both skills would prove lifesaving when, in 1897, Amundsen joined an expedition on the *Belgica* that attempted to study the South Magnetic Pole. Hired as first mate, Amundsen saved the captain and crew when they

The Arctic Circle is an imaginary line that lies 23.5 degrees south of the North Pole. It marks the northernmost point at which the Sun is visible at the winter solstice (December 22) and the southernmost point of the North Polar regions at which the midnight Sun can be seen.

became stuck in pack ice for over a year. At the worst point, as Amundsen wrote, ". . . we were . . . icelocked on every side by a complete circle of towering icebergs." When the captain and crew became ill, Amundsen insisted that the nutrition provided by eating seal and penguin meat could save them. He was right.

> **" I could never understand those people who were happy to kill for sport. "**

LIES AND LOSSES

After becoming the first to navigate completely through the Northwest Passage, he decided to try to be the first to reach the North Pole. When Americans Robert Peary and Frederick Cook claimed that success in April 1909, however, he decided to race Englishman Robert Scott to the opposite end of the Earth instead.

To win that race, he was even prepared to lie. He told the world — including his backers and crew — that he was heading to the *North Pole* to conduct scientific studies. That lie — plus his coldly calculated plan to kill half his sled dogs for food — tarnished his reputation.

He later lost a friendship after flying over the North Pole in the airship *Norge* with its Italian designer Umberto Nobile and American explorer Lincoln Ellsworth. The 16-man crew dropped Italian, Norwegian, and American flags at the North Pole and mapped this last unknown area of the world. Later, Amundsen and Nobile quarreled over who had contributed the most on the trip; but when Nobile radioed the world for help after his new airship the *Italia* crashed in the Atlantic in May 1928, Amundsen tried to rescue his estranged friend. Amundsen's aircraft never reached Nobile nor did it return. Amundsen's craft was later found, and he is presumed to have died in that plane crash at sea.

TIME LINE

1872
Roald Engelbreth Gravning Amundsen was born at Borge, Norway.

1893
Amundsen abandoned his medical studies when his mother died.

1897
Amundsen joined a Belgian expedition to Antarctica, aboard the *Belgica*.

1903-1906
Amundsen was first to navigate the Northwest Passage from the Atlantic to the Pacific Ocean.

1911
Having sailed to Antarctica in the *Fram*, Amundsen and his team reached the South Pole on December 14.

1918
Amundsen left Norway in the *Maud*, sailing to find a Northeast Passage.

1926
Amundsen flew in the airship *Norge* from Norway to Alaska over the North Pole — the first flight across the Arctic.

1928
Amundsen's airplane crashed into the Arctic while he was trying to rescue Italian aircraft designer Umberto Nobile.

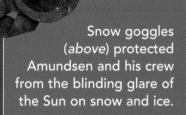

Snow goggles (*above*) protected Amundsen and his crew from the blinding glare of the Sun on snow and ice.

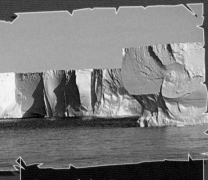

Parts of the Ross Ice Shelf cliffs (*above*) are over 100 feet (30 meters) high, yet they were scaled by Amundsen and his team.

These penguins (*below*) are well suited to life near the edge of an iceberg in Antarctica. Many polar explorers have found themselves less well equipped for this challenging terrain.

CHANGE OF DIRECTION

Amundsen's crew admired the way he carefully planned every detail of his expeditions, but for one voyage, he kept part of his plan a carefully guarded secret.

Norwegian explorer Fridtjof Nansen loaned his ship, the *Fram*, to Amundsen for a North Pole expedition. Then, as Amundsen himself described, ". . . just as everything was about ready, the world was electrified by the news that Admiral Peary, in April 1909, had reached the North Pole. This was a blow indeed! If I was to maintain my prestige as an explorer, I must quickly achieve a sensational success of some sort. I resolved upon a coup. . . ."

So Amundsen told the world he was going north for scientific research. Yet, as he confided to his brother Leon and the captain of the *Fram*, he was really heading to the South Pole instead.

But Captain Robert Scott, a British explorer who was also heading to the South Pole, was suspicious. Scott wrote to Nansen: "The fact that he departs with so much mystery leaves one with an uncomfortable feeling that he contemplates something which he imagines we should not approve."

Departing on June 7, 1910, Amundsen's crew thought they were headed for Alaska by going around the southern tip of South America. On September 6, the *Fram* stopped at the Madeira Islands, off the northwest coast of Africa. The crew was stunned when Amundsen then announced that they were heading for the South Pole.

ANOTHER WAY

Amundsen cabled Scott, after leaving Madeira, to say that their race to the South Pole was on. Both groups then wintered within 400 miles (644 kilometers) of one another, "to await the earliest practicable weather to attempt the dash to the Pole." To win, Amundsen needed to beat both Scott and the Antarctic climate. He believed his dogs and skis were faster than Scott's ponies and motorized sleds. He was right — the motors broke, and Scott's men had to haul their own supplies.

> "At six o'clock I called all hands on deck and announced my intention of heading for the South Pole."

Amundsen crossed the Ross Ice Shelf and climbed the Transantarctic Mountains at the Axel Heiberg Glacier. Scott's team took a longer route. Scott and his men reached the South Pole after Amundsen and his men and, tragically, died of starvation and cold on the way back to base camp.

CONQUERING ICE

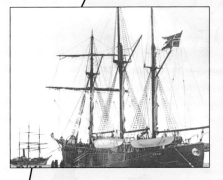

A ICE-WORTHY SHIP
Amundsen needed a tough, "ice-worthy" ship to take him to polar regions. Not every vessel can withstand the pressure of being hemmed in by hundreds of tons of pack ice. Many narrow-prowed iron ships belonging to other explorers had collapsed under the weight of ice, leaving their expeditions in ruins.

Ships also had to be seaworthy for world conditions. Until the Panama Canal was completed in 1914, there was no way for ships to get from the Atlantic to the Pacific except the long way. Without a Northwest (or Northeast) passage, that route was around the bottom of South America or Africa.

So Amundsen chose his vessels carefully. For example, he chose a triple-hulled Norwegian fishing vessel, the *Gjöa*, to conquer the Northwest Passage. For his journey to the South Pole, Amundsen persuaded Fridtjof Nansen to lend him his tried and tested *Fram* (*above left*). It had a rounded wooden bow that could take ice pressure.

He later chose the *Maud*, when he sought the Northeast Passage. Egg-shaped below the waterline, it could rise up over ice. An enthusiastic air pilot, Amundsen (*above*) also saw flight as a potential way to conduct polar voyages.

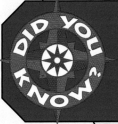

DID YOU KNOW?

The Antarctic Circle is an imaginary line that lies 23.5 degrees north of the South Pole. It marks the southernmost point at which the Sun is visible at the winter solstice (June 22) and the northernmost point of the South Polar regions at which the midnight Sun can be seen.

AMUNDSEN'S
ROUTE TO THE SOUTH POLE

After sailing for six months from the top of the world to the bottom, Amundsen set up camp at *Framheim* and prepared for his final trek. This map (*below*) shows the entire region inside the Antarctic Circle. The area immediately around the South Pole became known as King Haakon VII's Plateau and was named by Amundsen after the Norwegian ruler.

On December 14, 1911, Amundsen's team gripped the pole with "five weather-beaten frostbitten fists" and together planted Norway's flag at the South Pole.

SOUTH POLE

Amundsen left his tent at the South Pole along with pieces of his equipment, some fur clothes, and letters for the King of Norway and Captain Robert Scott.

ATLANTIC OCEAN

INDIAN OCEAN

GREATER (EAST) ANTARCTICA

Trans Antarctic Mountains

South Pole

Ross Ice Shelf

Axel Helberg Glacier

WEDDELL SEA

LESSER (WEST) ANTARCTICA

Antarctic Peninsula

Antarctic Circle

PACIFIC OCEAN

TRANS-

The first plane to land successfully at the South Pole was part of the United States Operation Deepfreeze 11, which took place in October 1956.

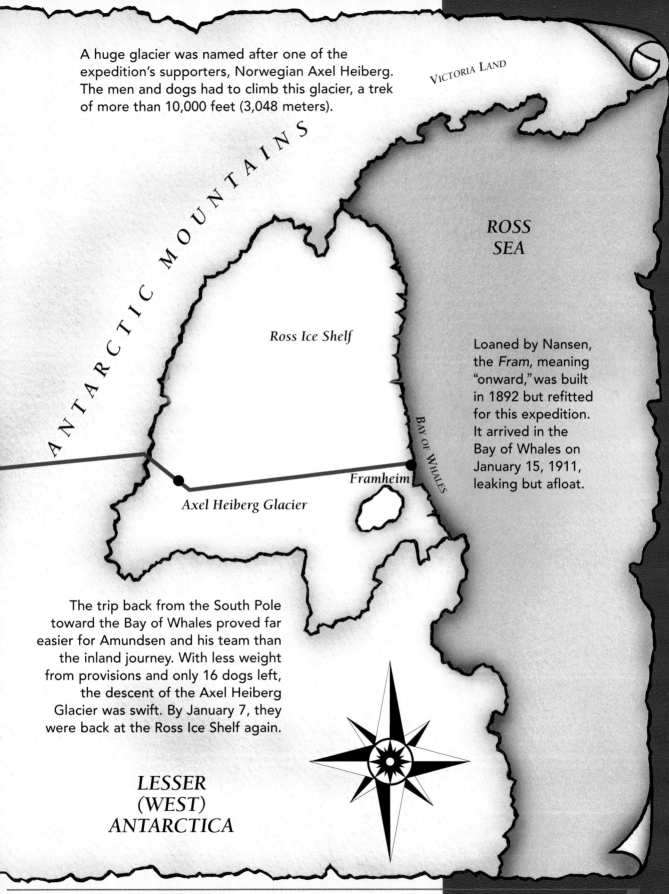

A huge glacier was named after one of the expedition's supporters, Norwegian Axel Heiberg. The men and dogs had to climb this glacier, a trek of more than 10,000 feet (3,048 meters).

VICTORIA LAND

ROSS SEA

Ross Ice Shelf

ANTARCTIC MOUNTAINS

BAY OF WHALES

Loaned by Nansen, the *Fram*, meaning "onward," was built in 1892 but refitted for this expedition. It arrived in the Bay of Whales on January 15, 1911, leaking but afloat.

Framheim

Axel Heiberg Glacier

The trip back from the South Pole toward the Bay of Whales proved far easier for Amundsen and his team than the inland journey. With less weight from provisions and only 16 dogs left, the descent of the Axel Heiberg Glacier was swift. By January 7, they were back at the Ross Ice Shelf again.

LESSER (WEST) ANTARCTICA

BY LAND, SEA, AND AIR

Some of Amundsen's crew tending to the *Fram's* sails (*above*). This vessel also had a diesel motor to use when the ship's speed fell too low.

Some members of the crew fished from the *Fram*. On one occasion, though, they caught an albatross (*above*) and kept the bird as a specimen to take with them back to Norway.

Members of Amundsen's crew used sextants (*right*). Navigational instruments of this kind played a vital role in keeping the expedition on course.

In his drive to succeed, Amundsen became a sea skipper, expert skier, mountain climber, dogsled driver, airplane pilot, and careful planner.

Amundsen, because he explored such remote, life-threatening climates, had to bring with him everything he would need, including wood to build his house and observatories. When he left timber to the Inuit after navigating the Northwest Passage, they were thrilled to have it. As Amundsen explained, "They did not possess a stick of their own;

and this gift meant to them an abundant supply of materials for the manufacture of sleds, spear handles, and other invaluable articles."

BRING YOUR OWN
Consequently, for each trip, the vessel was packed with equipment ". . . so that when we steamed into the Arctic Ocean we looked like a moving-van afloat!" Travels to the Antarctic required even more supplies than other destinations, because little more than microscopic life exists there. Unlike the Arctic, the Antarctic has no mammal life in its interior. The seals, penguins, and other

> *At every meal, we have to lash our chairs to the deck. . . . Not a moment's peace since we left Norway, except for the 2-3 days at Madeira.*

birds on its shores depend on the sea for food. Only two flowering plants have been found. Other than microscopic life, only moss, lichen, and insects exist inland.

So Amundsen made good use of space on the *Fram* to store what he needed for his sea and Antarctic travels. Men and dogs had to fit in where they could.

STORMY SEAS

The shallow keel of the *Fram*, specifically constructed to withstand pack ice, made the ship unstable. The men were used to a vessel tossing in treacherous waters, but the dogs were not. They often made it difficult to navigate, packing themselves together, shifting weight, and getting in the way on the bridge.

Accurate navigation was essential, and measurements were taken on the sextant several times a day. Storms had to be avoided because violent rolling might damage equipment, while stalling in windless waters would eat up vital time and supplies. Navigation through the ice floes in the Ross Sea would depend on Amundsen's highly skilled ice pilot, Andreas Peck.

POLAR FLIGHTS

After several grueling voyages, culminating in the *Maud* expedition that he left in the early 1920s, Amundsen turned his attention to a much easier method of getting to his most cherished destination, the North Pole. Amundsen earned his pilot's license in 1914 —the first civilian license issued in Norway. He had a plane stowed on the *Maud* at Alaska, intending to fly over his destination.

In Amundsen's first attempt at an air crossing of the Arctic in 1923, the craft crashed before he could embark. His second attempt, in an airplane supplied by U.S. millionaire Lincoln Ellsworth, came close to the Pole but had to crash-land on pack ice due to technical difficulties.

CARGO

Packing all the necessary equipment onto the *Fram* was not easy and took more than a month to complete. Each item was stowed in such a way that, when it came to unloading, every piece was available in the right order. The most important item for that expedition was the flat-packed hut for the party's winter quarters. Amundsen put a lot of thought into planning what cargo to take on his expeditions. In this photo (*below*), he is shown behind a sled filled with cargo prior to an expedition to the frozen north.

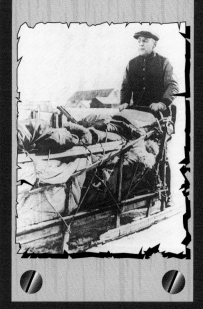

The vessel being unloaded (*right*) is the *Gjöa,* which Amundsen used for his voyage through the Northwest Passage and on which he spent almost his entire inheritance. Amundsen named the place where they dropped anchor *Gjöahaven.*

Onboard the *Maud,* Amundsen (*below*) would often relax by reading. The vessel was especially built for a journey to the Arctic and provided more room than most.

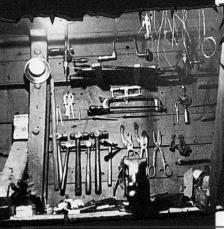

A corner of the engine room of the *Maud* (*left*), where essential tools were readily available in case the motor had to be repaired.

Determined to succeed, Amundsen now decided to try another method of flight that had recently become popular — the airship. This was a giant, gas-filled, cigar-shaped balloon with a cabin for crew and passengers bolted to the underside. He managed to get one from the Italian government (all airships belonged to the military at the time) and named it *Norge,* meaning "Norway." With its designer, Umberto Nobile, he flew over the North Pole on May 12, 1926. Once again, Amundsen was a hero in Norway. He decided it was time to retire.

AIRSHIP ACCIDENT

He spent the next two years lecturing worldwide to pay off his debts. In May 1928, he heard that Nobile had crashed in an airship while on a new venture to the North Pole. Even though he had previously quarreled with Nobile, because he felt the designer claimed too much credit for the successful flight of the *Norge,* Amundsen was the first to volunteer to try to save him.

> "*My ambitious dream was to fly from one continent to another over the Arctic.*"

Amundsen obtained an aircraft and pilot from the French government and took off from Tromsø, Norway, on June 18, searching over pack ice for the crashed *Italia.* Amundsen was never seen again. Nobile was rescued by others. Months later, Amundsen's aircraft wreckage was found, but there was no trace of Amundsen at all.

FIRST TO FLY OVER THE NORTH POLE

Originally, Richard Byrd claimed the honor of being

the first to fly over the North Pole, in 1926, just days before Amundsen's flight in the *Norge*. Recent research, however, reveals that Amundsen may truly have been the first. Observations in Byrd's diary, rediscovered in the archives of the Byrd Polar Research Center in Ohio, in 1994, strongly conflict with Byrd's official report. He appears to have turned back 149 miles (240 km) short of the Pole due to an engine leak, according to Dennis Rawlins, an expert in polar exploration who studied the diary.

This evidence means that Amundsen truly achieved a "first" at the North Pole. This dream was so dear to his heart that he said on

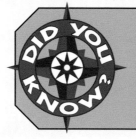

Amundsen and Oscar Wisting, who had been together on the successful South Pole expedition, became the first to reach both poles. This was a remarkable "first" for both men.

reaching the South Pole, "I have never known any man to be placed in such a diametrically opposite position to the goal of his desires as I was at that moment. The regions around the North Pole — well, yes, the North Pole itself — had attracted me from childhood, and here I was at the South Pole. Can anything more topsy-turvy be imagined?" He died not knowing that he had achieved his greatest dream.

Amundsen (*above*), dressed in flying gear of the period, before taking off in 1925 for the North Pole with Ellsworth. The venture failed, but they learned from the attempt and succeeded in flying over the pole in Nobile's *Norge* in 1926.

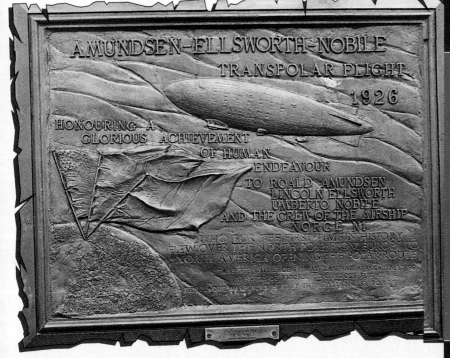

A memorial at Spitsbergen, Norway (*left*), commemorates the 1926 transpolar airship flight. The inscription reads, "Honoring a glorious achievement of human endeavor, To Roald Amundsen, Lincoln Ellsworth, Umberto Nobile, and the crew of the airship *Norge*, who for the first time in history flew over the North Pole from Europe to North America, opening the polar route."

The *Fram* (*above*) after overwintering at the Arctic in March 1895. Nansen, who owned the ship, let her freeze in place so she would drift in the pack ice, shortening the distance to be covered by men and dogs on their way to the North Pole.

A detail from a painting by E. Greenfield (*below*) shows an ice cave found on an early Antarctic expedition. The painting is based on a description of the terrain given by Ernest Shackleton. The explorer and his dog are dwarfed by the walls of ice.

ON FROZEN GROUND

The Antarctic challenged explorers with sudden crevasses, unmapped mountains, and cold so extreme that little life existed beyond the coasts.

Amundsen was determined to be the first man to reach the geographical South Pole, but he was grateful to the explorers who had been to the region of Antarctica before him. He used their information about the area to help him conquer this unknown territory.

EARLIER EXPLORERS

One explorer, Ernest Shackleton, had come within 97 miles (156 km) of the South Pole in 1909. Altitude sickness and lack of food on the polar plateau, which rises to over 11,000 feet (3,353 m), however, had forced him to turn back.

As far back as the 16th century, explorers knew this southern continent existed and called it *Terra Incognita*, or "unknown land." Later, during the 1770s, the British explorer Captain James Cook sailed around ice in the Antarctic Circle. But it was a Prussian named Fabian Bellingshausen, on a mission for the Russian Czar, who first sighted the land itself in 1820.

Explorers did not map the coast of Antarctica until the

> *All the crevasses were horrible . . . but we managed inch by inch, sledge length by sledge length.*

late 1830s. Most of the coast is sheer ice cliffs soaring up from the sea with few inlets where ships can land. The Transantarctic Range that defeated Shackleton was an unwelcome surprise when he came up against it, and explorers knew nothing about what lay beyond it.

Boldly, Amundsen decided the best place to drop anchor in Antarctica, January 15, 1911, would be the Bay of Whales. This was an inlet on the coast of the Ross Ice Shelf, which was named after a British explorer who had navigated these waters.

ON THE SHELF

It was called the Shelf because, while the rest of Antarctica is snow and ice covering a firm rock base, the Shelf is a floating block of ice attached to land. As the largest floating ice sheet in the world, it is about the size of France, approximately 213,000 square miles (551,670 sq km).

The Shelf is not a safe place. Huge chunks of it break off periodically in a process known as calving, so that yawning chasms many miles long and hundreds of feet deep are created. Crossing the Shelf when this is happening can cut explorers off from their base. Scott avoided the Ross Ice Shelf for this reason, preferring to start further away from the Pole, on firm ground; but Amundsen made a careful study of the Shelf and saw there had been no movement of ice during the previous 70 years. He therefore thought it was worth the risk.

Amundsen used this shelf to give him a 60-mile (97-km) advantage over Scott in their race to the South Pole. This provided a vital head start for Amundsen and his crew. It also proved to be warmer than Scott's land-based camp.

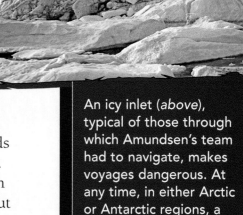

An icy inlet (*above*), typical of those through which Amundsen's team had to navigate, makes voyages dangerous. At any time, in either Arctic or Antarctic regions, a vessel can become stuck in the ice without much hope of rescue.

A recent photograph (*below*) shows a man shoveling snow away from his tent during a windstorm on Antarctica. Amundsen had to prepare for similar conditions.

CLIMATES OF THE POLAR REGIONS

THE SHIFTING RANGE OF THE ARCTIC
The Arctic region is not just the area enclosed by the Arctic Circle. Instead, it is defined by the shifting July isotherm (a map line that connects points of average equal temperature) that shows how far north trees are able to grow. So the Arctic region varies north and south of the Arctic Circle and generally includes the Arctic Ocean, the northern parts of Canada, Alaska, Russia, Norway, and the Atlantic Ocean, as well as Svalbard, most of Iceland, Greenland, and the Bering Sea.

This polar climate is divided by temperature into tundra (warmest temperatures below 50°F/10°C but above 32°F/0°C) and the ice cap climate with its permanent ice cover, where it never gets above freezing. The ice cap climate is very dry, but winds typically stir fallen snow to create the illusion of continuous snowfall. The tundra provides the only vegetation and has about twenty species of land animals, including moose, caribou, and reindeer, and six species of aquatic mammals, such as walrus, seals, and whales.

Coastal areas tend to be the warmest with heavier snows. The Arctic Ocean itself, the world's smallest ocean, surrounds the North Pole and remains frozen all year round except at its edges.

Sunlight varies seasonally with 24 hours of constant daylight or 24 hours of constant darkness.

The Arctic is one of the least populated areas of the world because of its difficult climate. It is home to people of Inuit, Lapp, Samoyede and Chuckchis ancestry and some Caucasian people in Siberia and Iceland. Inuit and northern Europeans live in Greenland.

THE VOLCANIC ANTARCTIC
This sixth-largest continent rests almost entirely within the Antarctic Circle, asymmetrically straddling the South Pole. Its two regions, Lesser Antarctica (a mountainous archipelago) and Greater Antarctica (a continental shield) are welded into a single continental mass by one thick ancient ice sheet. Over 95 percent of Antarctica is covered with ice. This ice is so thick that it buries entire mountain ranges, leaving only the tallest to emerge. Much of Greater Antarctica is near sea level, but the continent's dome, a snow-covered glacier, rises about 13,000 feet (3,962 m) above sea level. Volcanoes continue to be active in the region, and Antarctica is surrounded by the stormiest seas in the world. It has no native people. Little plant life and no animals exist in the interior.

A detail from a promotional collecting card of the period (*left*) shows flags flying as the airship *Norge* flies over the North Pole with Amundsen, Nobile, and Ellsworth on board.

Amundsen and Ellsworth brought this airplane (*above*) to the Arctic by sailing ship in a failed attempt to reach the North Pole.

Even though Amundsen did not notice movement of the Ross Ice Shelf, it is slowly but constantly on the move and floats northward at about 400 yards (366 m) annually. About every ten years, the front breaks off, and the pieces float to sea as enormous icebergs.

Amundsen's men dug deep ice corridors around Framheim (*above*), providing nature's own refrigerator for supplies.

Seals (*above*) sometimes wandered near Framheim and were killed for food.

An American flag at the Geographical South Pole (*right*). A 1961 Antarctic Treaty ensures goodwill in the region. Regular meteorological and other scientific work is now carried out here by many nations.

AT FRAMHEIM

There was no risk-taking, however, when Amundsen prepared for the killing Antarctic winter ahead. In Norway, he made a prefabricated building to create the party's main living quarters on the ice. He also brought tents for storage and dog kennels. The crew dug a warren of ice tunnels to keep their equipment and food safe from Antarctic winds.

> 66 *The land looks like a fairy tale . . . unseen and untrodden.* 99

By the time the Sun disappeared for the long winter nights in April 1911, Amundsen's *Framheim*, meaning "the home of *Fram*," was ready to shelter them until the South Polar spring of December, when they could travel again. The hut boasted the comforts of a linoleum floor, cork-lined walls, and a loft for insulation. This proved to be a lifesaver. By March, the building was up to its eaves in snowdrifts. The cook, Lindström, painted the ceilings white to give the cramped quarters the illusion of space.

DEVIL'S BALLROOM

Of all the hazards on Amundsen's trek, the most terrifying was a place his crew called the "Devil's Ballroom." There, what looked like a continuous sheet of ice extending for miles around was really horizontal layers of ice and snow that broke underfoot to reveal deep crevasses beneath. Time and again, the men and dogs crashed through this floor, saved only by their sled ropes.

The King and Queen of Norway wished Amundsen a safe journey when they visited the *Fram* (*above*) in 1910.

A WORTHY CREW

Amundsen handpicked his crew for their technical skills and ability to withstand the physical and emotional demands of seamanship and Antarctic exploration.

Amundsen took no chances with anything, and that included the men he chose for a crew to join him on his South Pole expedition. Each would need to prove his worth, both at sea and on the unmapped continent of Antarctica.

Hjalmar Johansen was the only member of Amundsen's expeditionary force who had as much experience in polar exploration as his leader. Johansen had worked with Amundsen's great hero, the renowned Norwegian explorer Fridtjof Nansen, famous as the first man to cross the Greenland ice cap in 1889. In fact, it was Nansen who first recommended Johansen to Amundsen, not only for his experience, but also for his skill at making scientific observations and as a dogsled driver. Unfortunately, Johansen disagreed publicly with Amundsen over weather conditions. He was transferred to another expedition.

Good food was assured when Amundsen chose Lindström (*above*) as the expedition's cook.

Breath steaming in the cold air, crew members Prestrud and Hanssen (*right*) tie wire around one of the many wooden cases in which provisions were carried.

COOKS AND SAILORS

Amundsen quite rightly observed that polar expeditions that failed often did so either because there was not enough food or because what food there was proved to be insufficiently nutritious to support men and beasts in a cold climate. So he chose the best cook he could find for his expedition. Adolf Lindström, who had been with Amundsen on the Northwest Passage voyage, could make a banquet out of the simplest ingredients. Favorite on the menu at base camp was seal steak. This tough meat was always served with Lindström's mouthwatering pastries, fruit tarts, and puddings. It was probably his skills at the stove that would make stringy dog cutlets easier for the men to swallow at the Axel Heiberg Glacier.

Another crew member, Helmar Hanssen, had previously sailed as a seal hunter, a skill that was to prove vital in obtaining fresh meat for the 800-mile (1,287- km) trek from the base camp to the South Pole. Hanssen was also skilled with metal and made tins to carry paraffin for heating.

Hanssen was exactly the kind of man Amundsen wanted to lead his dog teams. Amundsen had already seen him work on his voyage through the Northwest Passage. In fact, Amundsen had known Hanssen for 13 years. Hanssen's reserved nature made him a valuable crew member for the expedition. He succeeded in establishing food depots in dangerous weather conditions.

> ❝ *Honor to my faithful comrades who . . . helped to make our victory possible.* ❞

Also among the crew were Oskar Wisting, an excellent navigator and skilled dog handler, and Sverre Hassel, a master mariner with experience in the Antarctic. Good sailors, they worked among piles of boxes and sacks towering from floor to ceiling as the ship headed to the bottom of the world.

Fram's sailmaker, Martin Ronne, wrestled with his sewing machine as the ship pitched and tossed in choppy waters. He made everything, from bags to boots.

TEAM SPIRIT

It took a special blend of personalities to live together in cramped conditions for months on end, and Amundsen almost got it right on his South Pole expedition. Apart from his confrontations with Johansen, harmony reigned among his chosen men. Amundsen himself was thought of as a little unfeeling, but his men respected him for being firm but fair and called him "the Chief."

The men enjoyed their time together, but possibly because Amundsen kept them apart doing various tasks during the day. He even deliberately delayed much of the preparation for the South Pole trek until the last moment, so his crew would not be idle and have time to get on each other's nerves. This photograph (*below*) shows the whole crew onboard the *Fram* after their voyage to the South Pole.

Prestrud, during winter months at Framheim, is dressed in a hooded fur jacket and carries a dog whip (*right*), which he sometimes used to control the huskies.

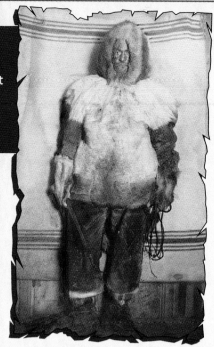

The *Fram's* chief engineer was a Swede named Knut Sundbeck (*above*). Amundsen described him as a genius and a shining example to all the crew.

Second mate on the *Fram* was Hjalmar Gjertsen (*left*), who had become inspired to go to sea by Viking legends he had read as a boy. Accounts of the adventures of many great explorers had influenced him, too.

CHIEF CALCULATOR

Also chosen for his navigational background was naval officer Lieutenant Kristian Prestrud. As a specialist in all aspects of navigation, he was charged by Amundsen with the task of making astronomical calculations and devising an accurate but simple method of finding a way over the polar ice. Since the interior of Antarctica had never been visited, no maps of this territory existed.

Prestrud was a jovial companion. It was his idea to name Amundsen's base camp Framheim. He also arranged a party in the main hut for those who had to stay behind on the vessel. During the long, cold nights, he taught English to his companions so they could read books written by earlier British explorers, such as Shackleton.

> *"The human factor is three-quarters of any expedition."*

CLEVER CARPENTER

Olav Bjaarland was a man of many talents. Not only was he the expedition's best skier, he was also a master carpenter. During the long Antarctic winter, which lasted from April 21 to August 24 in 1911 — the year Amundsen pitched base camp — it was Bjaarland's job to build sleds and make skis. Bjaarland made skis and sleds as strong as possible with the least amount of bulk and weight. This was crucial to the expedition's success. Lighter sleds and sleeker skis brought increased staying power and greater speed.

Bjaarland's skills were

also invaluable in helping construct the prefabricated building that became the landing party's refuge during those bitter months.

FINANCIAL SUPPORTERS

Amundsen was also helped by others who did not actually join any of his expeditions. Several wealthy supporters contributed to his expenses; and when he was in dire need of funds, the Norwegian Government gave him money to clear his debts and a grant for refitting the *Fram*.

The most essential help, inspiration, and guidance came from the Norwegian explorer Fridtjof Nansen, who loaned Amundsen his ship, the *Fram*, on the understanding that Amundsen had planned to go north.

When Nansen found out about the change of direction and learned how under-handed Amundsen had been, he was both resentful and shocked by the lie. This was hardly surprising. He had been planning to explore Antarctica himself, but he did not complain. Instead, he accepted that he had been cheated out of his ambition, simply stating, "If only he had told me, I could have assisted in so many ways."

Others, too, can be said to have helped Amundsen by providing inspiration — Sir John Franklin, for example, who had perished in an early attempt to navigate the Northwest Passage. As Amundsen wrote of Franklin, "A strange impulse made me wish that one day I would also go through the same sort of thing."

When the *Maud* became stuck on the Siberian coast during his Arctic expedition, Amundsen was grateful for Russian Gennady Olonkin's (*above*) help as an interpreter. No one else spoke the Russian language.

One of the crew on the *Maud* expedition to the Arctic proudly holds one of a pair of mammoth tusks (*right*) presented to Amundsen by a Russian trader. Mammoths, which became extinct many thousands of years ago, resembled huge elephants, and their tusks were a valuable commodity.

DEATH-DEFYING EXPLORERS

Each polar explorer, by contributing unique skills and strengths, has helped complete our map of the globe and increased our understanding of Earth.

This highly-decorative book cover (*above*) was designed for the 1911 Norwegian-language edition of Amundsen's *South Pole,* his own account of the journey.

Today it is clear that we owe these brave explorers and their dogs a debt of gratitude. Amundsen and other explorers of his time (with whom he both cooperated and competed) struggled against all odds to achieve something no one, in thousands of years of sailing and exploring the world, had been able to do. They conquered the most life-defying regions on Earth, the polar regions. In the process, they completed the map of our planet. This was achieved just a few decades before we were able to orbit Earth, fly to the Moon, set up space stations, and probe the planets of our Solar System. That they achieved these explorations in sailing ships and on dogsleds, with no calculators, telephone communication, or computerized navigational equipment, adds to our respect for their courage.

MULTI-TALENTED

Aside from their tremendous skills as seamen, outdoorsmen, leaders, and organizers, Amundsen and many of his fellow polar explorers had the ability to persevere. They trudged through killing cold and treacherous terrain. Perhaps equally difficult, they raised money for their

As with icebergs, whose tips just hint at their mass beneath the water, sailing ships hide much of their size while at sea. Next to the *Fram* (*left*), people seem tiny.

During each of his major voyages, Amundsen had to meet the most challenging conditions. Navigating past icebergs and rocky coastlines (*left*) was done under frequent threat of storms. So it is a tribute to the skills of the crews he selected that the vessels survived.

> ❝ *I was confident about placing our station on this part of the [Ross Ice] Barrier.* ❞

expeditions in times of political uncertainties that included war.

On their expeditions, the crew recorded numerous scientific observations. Amundsen and others wrote compelling books about their voyages. Their findings formed the basis of our understanding of Arctic and Antarctic climates, geology, and plant and animal life.

CALCULATED RISKS

Some of the so-called risks that Amundsen took were achieved after months of careful study of such things as the movement and calving rate of the Ross Ice Shelf. The Bay of Whales, in which he anchored, remained for only 50 more years and now no longer exists. He anchored in this temporary bay knowing from careful examination of coastal records of the area that the ice shelf was stable for the time being. As he explains in *My Life as an Explorer*,

Amundsen's men calculated the position of the geographical South Pole (*below*) and then traveled in a wide circle around it, just to be sure they had stood on this key ground.

DID YOU KNOW?

The geographical South Pole is different than the magnetic South Pole. The South Pole is the point of the Earth's axis, 90° south, a fixed point. The magnetic South Pole is not fixed but marks the southern end of our planet where Earth's magnetic intensity is greatest.

Amundsen's encampment at Framheim (*right*). The snow of the surrounding wall was often used for water.

> ❝*It is a marvel what the dogs did today, 17 nautical miles and a climb of 5,000 feet.*❞

In polar landscapes such as this (*above*), many explorers have met their death. Amundsen was fortunate and managed to survive the huge ice floes he encountered.

During the height of summer in either arctic or antarctic regions, the Sun shines 24 hours a day. Amundsen noted in a diary entry how splendid it was to see the midnight Sun (*right*).

"Our choice of a site for our base camp on the barrier (Shelf) was an essential factor in our success, just as Scott's choice of a site on the mainland to the west was an essential factor in his inability to return in safety from the Pole. In the first place, the air currents in the Antarctic regions make the weather much more severe on the land than on the ice. At best, the climate in the Antarctic is about the worst in the world, chiefly because of the terrific intensity of the gales which blow almost incessantly. . . . In his winter camp, Scott and his companions were harassed . . . with almost uninterrupted bad weather. . . . Our camp on the ice, however, was favored with infinitely better weather, and at no time were we subject to any discomfort."

UNIQUE GEOLOGY

The geology of the continent they explored is unique in the world. This made their progress over its surface truly challenging. They had no idea whether or not they could climb the unmapped mountains (with dogsleds and supplies, no less) and bridge the crevasses that riddled the snowcovered wastes. Volcanoes had been active in the region; perhaps it was better for their morale that they did not know this at the time.

Geologists have examined the fossils of plants, insects, animals, and fish found in Antarctica and believe that the two ice-bridged land masses of the Antarctica Continent, along with the other continents of the Southern Hemisphere, are part of an ancient supercontinent called Gondwanaland that crumbled prior to the Mesozoic era. Then, ages ago, the continents drifted to their present positions. Amazingly, these rocks explain the connection of the mountainous archipelago of West Antarctica to the Andes mountains of South America.

Antarctica is strewn with mountains and glaciers. It's highest peak is Vinson Massif at 16,864 feet (5,140 m).

Amundsen struck across the mountains and crossed the Axel Heiberg Glacier to get to the South Pole. He brought back about 20 specimens of rock from Mount Betty, and other members of his crew brought back rocks from, for example, Scott's Nanutuk, which was the only mountain clear of snow on their route to the South Pole. The lichen from these rocks was sent to Christiana University's Botanical Museum, while all rocks went to the University's Mineralogical Institute.

Bringing back specimens, when every ounce of weight was a burden, took determination. At times, the scant oxygen available in the mountains made the simplest movement exhausting. "The effect of the great and sudden change

of altitude made itself felt at once. When I wanted to turn around in my (sleeping) bag, I had to do it a bit at a time, so as not to get out of breath," Amundsen wrote.

Through it all, Amundsen's team kept their minds clearly on their goal, and at night, they recorded observations in their journals, preserving their progress step by step, crevasse after crevasse.

MASTERING THE CONTINENT

As Amundsen and his team trudged toward their goal, they had several narrow escapes. At one point, for instance, they were running blind in a blizzard. "I was afraid we might fall into a chasm before we could pull up," Amundsen wrote. They therefore decided to stop and wait until there was an improvement in the weather. When at last they were able to see, they found themselves just a few feet from the edge of a steep cliff.

They used scouts to ski ahead and open up trails for the dogsleds as they went. So trailblazers actually covered much of the same ground twice — blazing and then coming back to advise the team of their next steps.

Against all odds, they conquered the last uncharted continent on Earth.

WEATHER REPORT

When Amundsen finally set out for the South Pole on October 20, the weather seemed fair. The Sun dazzled on the endless snow, and the temperature was approaching warm. It was too good to last, though. Two days later, a blinding blizzard engulfed the party. They staggered across the Ice Shelf and often had to struggle out of treacherous crevasses. Pressing on, the team was rewarded by summer Sun at the beginning of November, just as they had ascended the Axel Heiberg Glacier. They now had a straight trek over the plateau.

Blizzards soon came back with a vengeance, however. For days, storms kept them at their final food depot. Then, as they pushed on to the Pole, the weather shifted. It was perfect when Amundsen finally reached the bottom of the world.

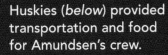

Huskies (*below*) provided transportation and food for Amundsen's crew.

TO THE DOGS!

Amundsen was bitter when the chairman of London's Royal Geographical Society proposed the above sarcastic toast at a dinner to honor his South Pole expedition.

A group of Amundsen's dogs resting at his first day camp in Antarctica, in 1911 (*above*).

Husky dogs had been used for centuries, by the Inuit and other native people of the Arctic regions, to get them across the frozen wastes of their homelands. Nansen suggested the dogs would help Amundsen in his polar explorations, as he had found them strong and helpful in the Arctic.

TRUSTY SERVANTS

In the winter of 1903–1904, Amundsen and his party had spent a great deal of time with the Netsilik Inuit of arctic Europe, learning to handle teams of husky dogs.

One of the dogs broke its leg while onboard the *Fram,* and two of the crew (*left*) set it.

The dogs made ideal work companions for the explorers. With good food (usually fish or seal meat) and enough rest, they could pull packed sleds through polar snows.

So dogs were key in Amundsen's plans for his expedition to the South Pole. One hundred were boarded on his vessel the *Fram* in Norway, although by the time the ship reached Antarctica, several more had been born to the pack.

Each member of the main expedition was assigned eight dogs to name and care for. The men grew so fond of them that they often gave some of their own rations to the huskies. To help the dogs manage on the long voyage southward, Amundsen

> ❝ *It hurts me to think that our faithful companions, our dear friends, will presumably all receive death as payment for faithful service.* ❞

Without Arctic huskies (*above*), Amundsen and his men might never have planted the Norwegian flag at the South Pole.

The dogs that got too thin on the voyage were fed butter from the crew's rations.

ordered that special laths should be nailed to the ship's decks so the dogs would have something to grip whenever the vessel rolled while at sea.

"Everyone," Amundsen wrote in his diary, "is looking after the dogs splendidly. . . . Dogs have rarely had such care. . . . The dogs are marvelous. We grow fonder and fonder of them each day. And this affection is mutual. They howl with delight every time they see us."

Some of the dogs became sick or had minor accidents during this expedition. One, for example, broke its leg, but some of the crew were able to set it.

The cook, meanwhile, had to be particularly careful when he went to get snow to thaw into water. So many dogs could foul a wide area around the camp, bringing risk of food poisoning if he used snow on which the dogs had relieved themselves.

MANAGING THE DOGS

While the men naturally expected certain hardships as the polar summer slipped into freezing winter, the dogs seemed baffled by it all. Used to the easy life aboard ship, they now reacted badly to being set down in the snow, only to be given exhausting work to do hauling cargo. They frequently snapped at each other and fought for no obvious reason, sometimes forcing Amundsen and his party to whip them into obedience.

Amundsen made sure that the dogs ate well so they would be able to do the work. As he wrote, "I shall try to feed them up properly before they go into harness. . . . They are now almost all big, round, and fat. I dare say they are at their best and raring to go."

As far as Amundsen was concerned, right from the start, the dogs had one purpose only — to ensure the success of the expedition. Amundsen was attached to them, but at the same time, he saw them as trained wild animals that had to be treated firmly. Huskies that disobeyed their drivers

This husky (*above*) is standing guard at the entrance to the hut at Framheim, Amundsen's base camp.

The strong husky dog (*left*), used by the Inuit to pull their sleds, is capable of speeds of 7–8 miles (11–12.8 km) per hour, so it can cover considerable distances in the course of a day.

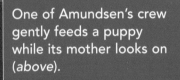

One of Amundsen's crew gently feeds a puppy while its mother looks on (*above*).

This recent photograph (*below*) shows a team of dogs pulling a sled near a British base in Antarctica. It illustrates the kind of weight these midsized dogs can pull with ease.

or fell seriously ill were shot, and their meat was then fed to the others.

SACRIFICING THE DOGS

Earlier in his life, Amundsen had always claimed he had no sympathy for those who killed animals for sport, but he was prepared to sacrifice some of his huskies for the sake of his expedition. His reasoning was that, "Having embarked on this record hunt, at all costs we had to be first. Everything had to be subordinated to the cause."

Yet not everyone around the world agreed that, in this instance, the end justified the means. Amundsen would be widely criticized for his apparent cold-blooded disregard for the lives of his team of dogs.

His plan had always been to shoot 24 of the dogs at a prearranged spot. He needed large dog teams to haul the sleds all the way up the mountain range that separates the Ross Ice Shelf from the polar plateau, but fewer were required for the expedition after that point. They could therefore be killed for food. As he explained in his book *My Life as an Explorer*, ". . . I was able to reduce the weight of provisions to be carried by calculating the flesh of the dogs which carried it as part of the food supply [for] us men. As there are about fifty pounds of edible food in the carcass of an Eskimo dog, it was quite probable that every dog we took south with us meant fifty less pounds of food be carried and cached. In my calculations before the start for the final dash to the Pole,

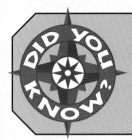

While onboard the *Fram*, the huskies were tied up at first and could not run about freely. Later, when they were let loose, the adults were muzzled so they would not start attacking each other too fiercely.

With the *Fram* in the background, Amundsen (*above*) takes a walk with his own dog, a St. Bernard. They were devoted to each other.

> " *It has been a hard day — mostly for the dogs. But twenty-four of our brave companions received the bitter wage — death. On arrival, they were shot.* "

I figured out exactly the precise day on which I planned to kill each dog as its usefulness should end from drawing the diminishing supplies on the sleds and its usefulness should begin as food for the men. This schedule worked out almost to the day and the dog. Above everything else, it was the essential factor in our successful trip to the Pole and our safe return to the base camp."

A practical outdoorsman, Amundsen's calculations shocked the dog-loving world. In contrast, while explorer Scott did not kill his ponies, his main expedition party all died and some just a few miles short of returning to base camp.

All the men were almost in tears as they shot the dogs, and most could barely bring themselves to eat the flesh at first. In the end, however, the dogs themselves were hungry enough to eat the entrails. The spot where they slaughtered the dogs would always be known as the "butcher's shop."

Sometimes members of Amundsen's team would go along on skis (*above*) while the dogs pulled sleds piled with supplies and special equipment.

The Norwegian polar explorer Fridtjof Nansen (*left*), known as the "father of modern day polar exploration," first suggested the use of huskies to Amundsen.

THE NORTHWEST PASSAGE

For centuries before Amundsen found a route through the Arctic, many ships had tried to find a shortcut to the eastern world (*above*).

A hut built in the Arctic by the Dutch explorer William Barents (*below*) in 1597. He, too, had tried to find the Northwest Passage and in the attempt became the first European to survive an Arctic winter.

Many explorers struggled to find a passage through the Arctic to get from one ocean to another without going around South America or Africa.

Ambition struck Amundsen at around age 17 when Fridtjof Nansen returned to Norway, a hero for crossing Greenland. Nansen inspired Amundsen to find the fabled seaway to the East through Arctic waters. Amundsen said, "As I walked among the flags and cheering, all my youthful dreams came to the fore. For the first time, in my secret thoughts, I heard an insistent whisper: If you could do the Northwest Passage!"

For over 400 years, traders had hoped an explorer would succeed in locating this shortest route to Asia. They wanted to find a sea route through the huge joined continents of North and South America or, possibly, Europe and Africa. They needed a route that did not force them to go around Cape Horn, at the tip of South America, or across the difficult waters of the Cape of Good Hope, at the bottom of Africa. The Panama Canal,

> ❝ *The Northwest Passage was therefore open to us. But our first task was to obtain exact data about the Magnetic North Pole.* ❞

which now provides a passage from one ocean to another through Central America, would not be built until 1904–1914. This search for a shortcut was a driving force behind the exploration of North America.

OVER THE TOP

Some explorers tried to go over the top of Europe and Asia to create a Northeast Passage. Others, like the Hudson's Bay Company, chartered in 1670 by Charles II of England to find a passage "to the Orient," took a century before discovering, with British explorer Samuel Hearne, that there is no Northwest Passage through continental North America. After that, explorers focused their efforts on literally "going over the top" of the Arctic Circle to find a different Northwest Passage.

By the mid-1800s, connected water routes through the Arctic archipelago of northern Canada and the northern coast of Alaska linking the Pacific and Atlantic Oceans

were found to exist, but no one had been up to the challenge of getting through them. Since it seemed too difficult to be useful, merchants and governments became less interested in funding expeditions for this physically shorter but ice-choked route.

SECRETS OF SCIENCE

Amundsen, seriously short of money, did not feel he would be supported in his goal to find a Northwest Passage.

Martin Frobisher tried to find the Northwest Passage in 1577 but fought with Inuit natives (*above*) and was forced to turn back.

Another English Explorer, William Edward Parry, (*above*) tried to get through the Northwest Passage in 1819–1820 but did not succeed.

This medal (*left*) was awarded to Sir John Franklin in 1846 by King William IV. Franklin had disappeared on a voyage to find the Northwest Passage, but his efforts were an inspiration to Amundsen.

During his search for the Northwest Passage as well as on other expeditions, Amundsen came across a wide variety of Arctic animals, some of which are shown in a painting (*right*) that dates from 1903. Many mammals, amphibians, birds, and insects are dependent on the Arctic tundra for all or part of their life cycle.

Amundsen (*below*) learned how to dress for maximum warmth from the Inuit people he met during his voyage through the Northwest Passage.

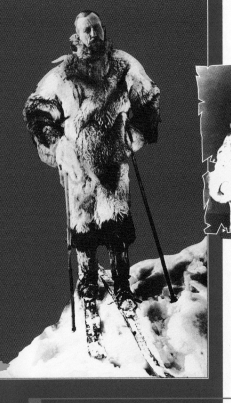

So, just as he did later when he said he was going to the North Pole but really raced to the South Pole, Amundsen kept his purpose a secret. Again, he gave a different reason for setting sail.

He knew that the North Magnetic Pole lay in the region where he had the best hope of finding a

Taken in 1925, a photograph (*above*) shows Amundsen with Inuit children he brought with him to visit Norway. He had great admiration for the Inuit culture.

Northwest Passage. He hoped he could locate and study the North Magnetic Pole and become the first to cross the Northwest Passage at the same time.

He thought a scientific goal might help him find investors. So he claimed that the North Magnetic Pole was of great interest to him, but he did not stress his interest in the Northwest Passage. His career-long tendency of keeping secrets and telling lies was beginning.

At this point, his creditors were threatening to seize the *Gjöa*, his ship on which he had spent his entire inheritance. Just in time, some private investors were found to help support what they thought would be a study of the North Magnetic Pole. To set sail, he had to escape his creditors by boarding the *Gjöa* in secrecy.

In April 1904, Amundsen began to earn his financial support by looking for the Magnetic North Pole. Explorers did not know it then, but, because it is subject to Earth's shifting magnetic currents, it is not a fixed point. It had been

recorded in 1831 by Sir James Ross to be on King William Island, but Amundsen discovered on arrival that it had moved! At least he would have that scientific data to report to his investors. He had found that "In the evening we could be quite near the (North Magnetic Pole). . . . But next morning the needle swung far off." These findings confirmed his suspicions that the magnetic poles are not exact and gave him important scientific data.

He then successfully navigated the Northwest Passage through the treacherous icy channels that twist between Canada's mainland and the many Arctic islands — a double victory for Amundsen.

While wintering during this voyage, he sold exclusive rights to his story to certain newspapers. Unfortunately, a cable outlining the story was pirated by some members of the U.S. press. So his deal was off, and his plan to pay off his creditors with the profits was ruined.

INUIT INFLUENCE

Happily, during this voyage from 1903 to 1906, Amundsen became friendly with the Inuit and learned much about their customs. He admired their skills and wrote, "to me it was wonderful to see the artistic sense. . . . The women are very adept at cutting out the black parts and the white parts of the caribou skins and fashioning them into beautiful shapes. . . . Their bead work, too, made from the teeth and . . . dried bone of the caribou, showed taste and skill." He also learned techniques from the men that helped him survive in the wild. He was taught to line his boots with felt and grass for insulation.

Now that he had received his Inuit education, Amundsen's contributions to science and the mapping of the world had truly just begun. The U.S. explorer Adophus Greely said Amundsen's voyage proved him to be "a man endowed with high qualities of administration, judgment, and resourcefulness."

IN THE WAKE OF HIS SHIP

- The Inuit people were greatly harmed by Western cultural influences that came with the exploration of their homelands. Subjected to forced relocation, they now have a degree of self-government and mostly live in a semi-independent region of Canada known as Nunavut.

- Since Amundsen's first journey through the Northwest Passage, this route has been followed by other ships, steel yachts, icebreakers, cruisers, and submarines. The discovery of natural resources in Arctic regions has encouraged new settlements.

- It is possible that the route will be used more frequently in the future as sea-going technology improves. In the past, ships that got trapped in the Arctic ice had to resort to using explosives to blast their way out of the situation.

POLAR EXPLORERS

British explorer Robert Falcon Scott (*above*) was beaten to the South Pole by Amundsen but is still highly regarded.

The "golden age of polar exploration" inspired many to compete to become the first, but the controversy over who really came in first continues.

A hut (*above*) that belonged to Scott survives as a memorial to him at McMurdo Station in Antarctica. Scott died trying to return from the South Pole through a blizzard.

Not everybody went wild with delight when news of Amundsen's South Pole success reached the outside world on March 7, 1912. The British particularly felt cheated. As the leading maritime nation, they felt it was British explorer Robert Falcon Scott who deserved the prize — not this upstart Norwegian Roald Amundsen, who had deceived the world about his intentions in the first place.

Furthermore, Amundsen had coldly planned to sacrifice the lives of his animals for his ambition. The British generally believe in "playing the game by the rules." Planning to eat the dogs that pulled his own sleds was not, in their code, fair play. Scott's party, on the other hand, only shot their ponies in extreme circumstances, then dragged the supply sleds themselves. The sense of outrage over the details of Amundsen's voyage could not erase, however, the fact that Scott arrived at the South Pole on January 18, 1912 — over a month after Amundsen's party had arrived on December 14, 1911 — only to find a Norwegian flag and a welcoming letter.

This detail of a painting (*left*) is in the collection of the Scott Polar Research Institute in Cambridge, England. It shows a sled being hauled by men.

> 66 *What courage, what tenacity, had been shown in the fight against cold, hunger and hardships.* 99

Ernest Shackleton (*above*) came within 97 miles (156 km) of the South Pole in 1909, not long before Amundsen.

SOUR GRAPES

This meant that Amundsen angered many people in Britain for coming back alive and well. Some could not accept that this man, a Norwegian and a citizen of a country only a few years old at the time, could have beaten their nation in this race to the South Pole.

As Amundsen himself noted in his autobiography, "The year after my journey to the pole, the son of a prominent Norwegian living in London came home to his father and protested against learning at school that Scott had discovered the South Pole. On looking into this, it was found the boy was right, and that it was usual for other [British] schools to ignore the Norwegian expedition."

SOUTH POLE FIRSTS

In fact, the list of explorers who vied to be first at either pole — whether by dogsled, ship, airplane, or snow-tractor — shows that many explorers competed to get their names in the history books. British explorers Robert Scott and Ernest Shackleton had already made inroads into the continent of Antarctica when the race began seriously, but neither had reached the Pole itself. The final list of those who made it to the South Pole includes these "firsts":

The hut that belonged to Shackleton (*above*) is preserved at Ross Island, Antarctica, to this day.

A group of polar explorers, among them Johansen, Nansen, and Amundsen (*left*), in 1895, sharing information in the "golden age of polar exploration."

A hero's welcome awaited Amundsen and Ellsworth when they got back to Oslo, Norway, in 1926 (*above*).

Seen with a group of potential sponsors (*below*), Amundsen was an excellent self-publicist.

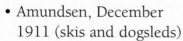

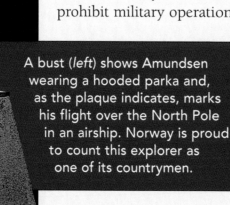

A bust (*left*) shows Amundsen wearing a hooded parka and, as the plaque indicates, marks his flight over the North Pole in an airship. Norway is proud to count this explorer as one of its countrymen.

- Amundsen, December 1911 (skis and dogsleds)
- Scott, January 1912 (motorized sleds and ponies)
- Byrd, November 1929 (airplane)
- Dr. Vivian E. Fuchs, January 1958 (snowtractor)

Evolving from competition to cooperation, a scientific village is now maintained by the United States at McMurdo, Antarctica, for international scientific study. Some important findings from there include the discovery of ozone depletion, or "holes," in the stratosphere over the Antarctic. This lets harmful ultraviolet rays reach Earth and may cause dangerous global warming.

Today, international cooperation in Antarctic studies plays a key role in global decisions, as we are challenged to protect our environment. International agreements, dating from the Antarctic Treaty of 1959, prohibit military operations and territorial claims by any nation and provide for freedom of scientific investigation in Antarctica.

NORTH POLE FIRSTS

Competition continues at the North Pole, as controversy over who was truly first to fly over it rekindles. The official list of those who made it to the North Pole first includes the following:

- Peary, April 1909 (dogsleds), unsuccessfully contested by Frederick Cook
- Byrd, May 1926 (airplane), or Amundsen based on new information that questions the accuracy of Byrd's records
- Amundsen, Ellsworth, and Nobile, May 1926 (airship)
- William R. Anderson, August 1958 (US *Nautilus* — the first atomic powered submarine)

Many of these explorers were inspired by Fridtjof Nansen. After becoming the first to cross Greenland, he went on to become Norway's first minister to Britain and won a Nobel Peace Prize for rescuing famine-stricken Russian refugees. Amundsen, Shackleton, and Scott credit Nansen with inspiring them to push on to explore the coldest areas on Earth — the polar regions.

FOR FURTHER DISCUSSION

Many aspects of Amundsen's travels are thought to be controversial and therefore open to debate. The following questions can be used to guide classroom discussion.

1 Should Amundsen have kept everyone in the dark about his plan to head toward the South Pole? What other secrets did he keep, and why?

2 Was Amundsen right to kill many of his dogs for food? Should he have made other plans for feeding his crew?

3 Dog meat is not generally eaten in the West, but in some parts of the world it is acceptable. Do you like the idea of eating dog meat?

4 If you were given the job of planning a new memorial for Amundsen, what form would it take? Where would you place it?

5 Why do you think that dogs made better work animals than ponies for a journey to the South Pole? Where did Amundsen get these dogs, and how did he learn to handle them?

6 Why were the people of Great Britain so reluctant to recognize Amundsen's team as the first to reach the South Pole?

7 Many forms of transportation have been used in arctic exploration. What are the advantages and disadvantages of each?

8 What forms of communication were available to Amundsen during his arctic travels?

9 Which parts of the terrain of the Antarctic were the most dangerous, and why?

10 To whom should Amundsen have been most grateful for his success in reaching the South Pole?

11 What skills did the Inuit people of the Arctic share with Amundsen? How did these skills help him survive?

12 What were the key skills that Amundsen's South Pole crew brought to the expedition? Why were these skills important?

13 Which explorers do you think Roald Amundsen most admired, and why?

14 Why was the Northwest Passage so difficult to find and navigate?

15 What are some special features of ships that allow them to push through ice?

MAJOR WORLD EVENTS

During the time Roald Amundsen was exploring uncharted places, people in the rest of the world were showing off new inventions, as well as struggling with war.

Find out about some of these major world events (*right*), and judge how they may have affected Amundsen's accomplishments.

1901 Marconi's first transatlantic wireless message was sent from England to Newfoundland, which is now a part of Canada.

1903 The first sustained flight by a power-driven plane was made by Wilbur and Orville Wright in the United States.

1906 The Pogroms, during which Jews were murdered, were still taking place in Russia when Amundsen navigated the Northwest Passage.

1908 The first mass-produced car, the Model T, came off the assembly line, followed by 18 million more by 1927.

1910 The takeoff of the first seaplane, invented by Frenchman Henri Fabre, succeeded.

Combat in the trenches during World War I (*above*).

1910 Research on crystals, done by Americans Dunwoody and Pickard, led to the invention of the first radio.

1904–1914 The Panama Canal was built to allow passage from the Atlantic to the Pacific Oceans.

1914–1918 World War I was waged with the largest armies ever seen up to that time. For the first time, airplanes and airships were used in combat.

1918 The Russian Czar and his family were massacred during the Russian Revolution.

The Wright brothers (*left*) tested out their plane in North Carolina in 1903.

OVER THE YEARS

- There is a Roald Amundsen Center for Arctic Research at the University of Tromsø, Norway.

This portrait of Amundsen (*left*) is based on existing photographs of the explorer.

- In November 1999, NASA announced that two microprobes of the Deep Space Two Mission, scheduled to reach the south of Mars, would be named after Amundsen and Scott.

- Amundsen has been honored by giving his name to a sea, a gulf, and a bay.

- The *Fram* Museum, named after the ship Nansen loaned to Amundsen, was opened in Oslo, Norway, in 1935 and now welcomes 250,000 visitors every year.

- A commemorative silver medal and a coin were struck by the Royal Norwegian Mint in 1995 to mark the 60th anniversary of the *Fram* Museum.

- At the Amundsen-Scott South Pole Station in Antarctica, scientists carry out research and live together for several months at a time inside a geodesic dome.

- There are, around the world, several copies of a larger-than-life bronze bust of Amundsen. Originally sculpted by American artist Alonzo Lewis, one is located at Spitzbergen, Norway; another is in Nome, Alaska; a third is in Hobart, Tasmania; and a fourth is in Nunavut, Canada, the semi-independent homeland of the Inuit who were known to have given Amundsen much advice about how to survive in a polar environment.

- A rock structure, known as "Amundsen's Cairn," can be seen on the Queen Maud Range of the Antarctic Mountains. It was erected by Amundsen himself, when he was on his way back to Framheim after reaching the South Pole, as a sign that he had indeed reached this remote and inhospitable region of Antarctica.

Although many people questioned his methods and his tendency to keep secrets, Roald Amundsen developed great skills on land, in sea, and in the air, as well as achieving historic success at both poles.

Discover how some of his achievements have been remembered (*left*).

GLOSSARY

airship: a mechanically driven aircraft that is carried by a lighter-than-air balloon.

altitude sickness: nosebleeds, nausea, or other symptoms caused by a lack of sufficient oxygen at high elevations.

archipelago: a group of islands or an area of sea containing many islands.

autobiography: a book written by a person about his or her own life.

cairn: stones piled up as a memorial or landmark.

calving: the breaking up of a glacier into icebergs.

chasm: a deep opening in the earth or ice.

commodity: something useful or of value.

coup: a sudden and successful act.

crevasse: a deep opening in a glacier.

czar: the former name for a ruler of Russia.

depot: a place for storing supplies.

diametrically: being at opposite extremes.

expedition: a journey taken for a specific purpose.

geodesic dome: a rounded structure made of many straight bars. Strong and lightweight, it needs no supports inside to hold it up.

glacier: a large body of slowly moving ice.

global warming: a warming of Earth's temperatures due to holes in the atmosphere that allow in excessive ultraviolet rays.

hemisphere: a half-sphere, or half of the globe divided through the center, either at the equator (to make northern and southern hemispheres), or at a meridian (to make eastern and western hemispheres).

ice floe: a large sheet of ice floating on the surface of a body of water.

iceberg: a huge mass of floating ice.

inhospitable: showing no friendliness.

Inuit: a group of native people from Arctic regions, also called Eskimo.

keel: the part of a ship running front to back that supports its frame and extends beneath, like a fin, aiding in balance.

laths: thin strips of wood.

lichen: plants, made up of algae and fungus, growing on a surface.

magnetic pole: In the North and South Polar regions, direction indicated by the needle of a magnetic compass attracted to where the magnetic pull is most intense.

maritime: relating to navigation of the sea.

merchants: buyers and sellers of goods.

Mesozoic: a time in Earth's history when dinosaurs existed.

meteorological: concerning the atmosphere of Earth and its weather.

microscopic life: creatures so small that they are invisible without the use of a microscope.

midnight Sun: the condition that exists when the Sun is visible at midnight during the summer in Arctic or Antarctic regions; caused by the seasonal tilt of Earth on its axis.

Northeast Passage: a water route leading from the Atlantic to the Pacific along the northern coast of Europe and Asia.

Northwest Passage: a water route leading from the Atlantic to the Pacific along the northern coast of mainland Canada and Alaska.

ozone: a form of oxygen naturally occurring in Earth's atmosphere that absorbs and protects the planet from excessive ultraviolet radiation.

pack ice: large floating pieces of ice driven together by winds and water currents.

paraffin: a colorless waxy or liquid mixture used for candles and heat.

pemmican: a nutritious food made from dried meat, which is mixed with fat and berries or dried fruit and pressed into small cakes.

pirated: referring to a person's production, invention, or concept that is used without his or her permission.

plateau: a large area of flat land raised above surrounding land.

prefabricated: prepared in advance so that pieces can be easily assembled later.

sextant: a scientific instrument for measuring angular distances and generally used by navigators for determining their position.

stratosphere: a part of Earth's atmosphere that extends 7–31 miles (11–50 km) above the surface.

subordinated: treated as being less important or of a lesser value.

terrain: landscape or type of land.

topography: the physical or natural features of a surface or landscape.

traders: people whose business it is to buy and sell goods.

uncharted: unknown territory not plotted on a map.

FOR FURTHER STUDY

BOOKS

Antarctic Journal: Four Months at the Bottom of the World. Jennifer Owings Dewey (HarperCollins)

DK Discoveries: Polar Exploration. Martyn Bramwell (DK Publishing)

Destination — Polar Regions. Jonathan Grupper (National Geographic Society)

Endurance: Shackleton's Perilous Expedition in Antarctica. Meredith Hooper (Abbeville)

Four to the Pole: The American Women's Expedition to Antarctica, 1992–1993. Nancy Loewen (Shoe String Press)

Great Polar Adventures: The Journey of Roald Amundsen. Andre Langley (Chelsea House Publishing)

Matthew Henson and the North Pole Expedition. Ann Gaines (Child's World)

Over the Top of the World. Will Steger (Scholastic)

Peary and Amundsen: Race to the Poles. Antony Mason (Raintree Steck-Vaughn)

Shipwreck at the Bottom of the Sea. Jennifer Armstrong (Random House)

Women Explorers in Polar Regions. Margo McLoone (Capstone Press)

Worst Journey in the World: Antarctic, 1910–13. Apsley Cherry-Garrard (Pan Books, Ltd.)

VIDEOS

Glory and Honor. (Warner Home Video)

National Geographic: Antarctica: Life in the Freezer. (Questar, Inc.)

National Geographic's Antarctica: The Last Wilderness. (Questar, Inc.)

Shackleton: Escape from Antarctica. (Kultur Video)

WEB SITES

National Geographic Xpeditions. **www.nationalgeographic.com/expeditions**

Virtual Antarctica at Terra Quest. **www.terraquest.com/va/index.html**

Global Warming Kids Site from the United States Environmental Protection Agency. **www.epa.gov/globalwarming/kids**

Arctic Exploration Online from NASA and the United States Coast Guard. **www.quest.arc.nasa.gov/arctic**

Think Quest. **library.thinkquest.org/26442/html/index.html**